D0569418

MAMMALS

A TRUE BOOK

by
Melissa Stewart

Children's Press®
A Division of Grolier Publishing

New York London Hong Kong Sydney
Danbury, Connecticut

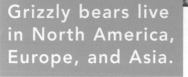

Grizzly bears live
in North America,
Europe, and Asia.

Content Consultants
Kathy Carlstead, Ph.D.
National Zoological Park
Smithsonian Institution
Washington, D.C.

Jan Jenner, Ph.D.

Author's Dedication
For Dave,
my favorite mammal

The photograph on the cover
shows a tiger resting.
The photograph on the title
page shows a group of
African elephants.

**Visit Children's Press® on
the Internet at:
http://publishing.grolier.com**

Library of Congress Cataloging-in-Publication Data

Stewart, Melissa.
    Mammals / by Melissa Stewart.
        p. cm. — (A true book)
    Includes bibliographical references and index.
 Summary: Describes the basic behavior, physical traits, and life cycles of
mammals, including humans.
ISBN: 0-516-22035-7 (lib. bdg.)   0-516-25952-0 (pbk.)
    1. Mammals—Juvenile literature. [1. Mammals.] I. Title. II. Series.
QL706.2 .S75   2001
599—dc21   99-057898
                                                                           CIP
                                                                            AC

©2001 Children's Press®,
A Division of Grolier Publishing Co., Inc.
All rights reserved. Published simultaneously in Canada.
Printed in the United States of America.
1 2 3 4 5 6 7 8 9 10 R 10 09 08 07 06 05 04 03 02 01

GROLIER
PUBLISHING

Contents

Horses (top) use their legs to run. Spotted dolphins (above) use their flippers to swim. Squirrel monkeys (right) use their arms and legs to climb.

What Is a Mammal?

Cheetahs and horses run across the land. Whales and dolphins swim in the ocean. Bats fly through the air. Monkeys climb in the trees. Prairie dogs burrow in the ground. Mammals are everywhere. In fact, one kind of mammal has even walked on the Moon.

Believe it or not, you belong to the same group of animals as cows and kangaroos, hippos and hares, mice and muskrats. There are so many different kinds of mammals in the world that you might have trouble figuring out what they all have in common.

All mammals have a backbone that supports their body and helps them move. They also have lungs and

Although they live in different regions, the arctic hare (top) and the hippo (bottom) are both mammals.

Most female cheetahs give birth to three to six cubs. This cheetah is feeding five cubs.

breathe air. They are warm blooded, so their body temperature stays the same no matter how cold or warm it is around them. Female mammals give birth to babies and feed them milk. Most mammals have four legs and hairy bodies.

Thick, black hair covers most of this gorilla's body.

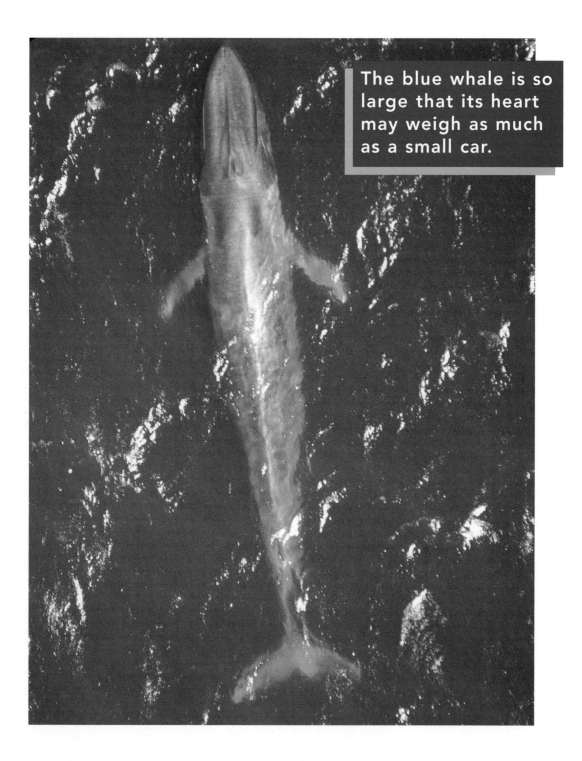

The blue whale is so large that its heart may weigh as much as a small car.

Mammals come in all shapes and sizes. The blue whale is the largest mammal that ever lived on Earth. It may be up to 108 feet (33 meters) long and weigh 210 tons. The smallest mammal, Kitti's hog-nosed bat, is the size of a bumblebee and weighs as much as two paperclips.

Where Mammals Live

Mammals live on every continent and in every ocean on Earth. No matter where a mammal lives, it has special features that help it survive. A layer of fat and thick fur help a polar bear survive in the cold north. A kangaroo rat avoids the desert heat by

A layer of fat keeps the polar bear warm and allows it to go for weeks without eating.

A kangaroo rat stores food
in its cheek pouches.

hunting at night and resting during the day. It needs little water, and its body loses heat easily.

Over time, the arms and legs of some mammals have changed to help them survive. A human stands on two legs and can use his or her arms to hold and carry objects. A bat has flaps of skin attached to its long fingers, so it can fly through the air. Whales, dolphins, seals, and walruses are

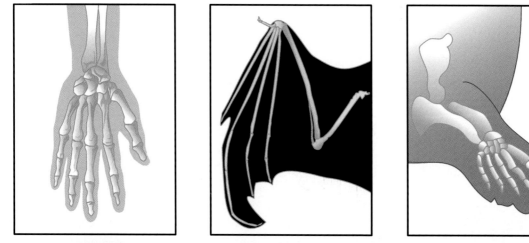

Human   Bat   Walrus

Even though a person's hand, a bat's wing,
and a walrus's flipper look very different,
the bones inside the animals are very similar.

such good swimmers because
they have flippers instead of
legs. Ocean mammals have
little or no hair. A layer of
fatty blubber keeps them
warm and helps them float.

Facts About Food

Mammals eat all kinds of food. Some eat animal meat. Others eat plants. Still others eat meat and plants. You can usually tell what a mammal eats by looking at its teeth.

Coyotes, leopards, and foxes have long canine teeth

These gray wolves are using their sharp teeth to eat a deer.

so they can grab prey and
sharp molars to slice flesh.
Zebras, horses, cows, giraffes,
and rhinos have teeth that
help them tear and grind

The giraffe grasps tree leaves with its tongue and chews them with its teeth.

tough grasses. Mice have teeth perfectly designed for gnawing seeds and nuts. The teeth of moles and shrews are useful for eating insects.

The first food that any mammal has is its mother's milk. Almost all baby mammals grow inside their mothers until they are ready to be born. A mammal mother often gives birth to many babies at once. Some mice have litters with as many as eighteen babies.

Most newborn mammals are completely helpless. They have no teeth and no fur. Many are blind and deaf. For several weeks, months, or

These helpless newborn mice do not have fur and cannot see.

years, young mammals cannot survive without help from their parents. Newborns suck milk from their mother's mammary glands. Dog pups drink mother's milk for about 6 weeks, while lion cubs nurse for about 2 months and elephant calves nurse for up to 2 years. A baby whale can drink 3 gallons (11 liters) of milk in just 5 minutes and may feed 40 times a day. That's a lot of milk!

Milk—It Does a Body Good

Milk is truly the perfect food for babies. It gives them everything they need to stay strong and healthy. Milk is made up of water, sugar, protein, fat, and vitamins and minerals. The sugar gives babies energy. The proteins make milk look white and cloudy. They are used to build body parts as babies grow. The fat helps babies store extra food and energy. The vitamins and minerals keep babies' bones strong and eyes sharp. They also help fight some diseases.

Humans drink milk from a variety of other mammals, including cows, goats, and llamas.

The Importance of Hair

All mammals have some hair on their bodies. Bears and foxes are covered with thick coats of fur. Even whales and elephants have some hair.

For most mammals, hair keeps heat in and cold out. Hair also protects mammals from the sun and wind. Fur

The arctic fox's thick, white fur keeps it warm and hides it from predators.

helps make it possible for mammals to live in so many different parts of the world.

Hair comes in many different colors, textures, and forms. A rabbit's fur helps it hide from enemies. A giraffe's long eyelashes protect its eyes from dirt and flying objects. A cat uses its whiskers to sense its surroundings. A lion uses the tuft of hair on its tail to shoo flies and other insects.

The eastern cottontail rabbit's brown fur blends in with its surroundings.

Long, sharp hairs grow together to form a porcupine's needlelike quills.

A porcupine's sharp quills are also a kind of hair. They keep the animal safe from predators. A rhino's horns are made of tightly packed hairs.

A rhino's horns are made of the same material as human hair and fingernails.

They are so tough that they can poke holes through metal. Polar bears and caribou live in the far north. They have hollow hairs that trap extra heat to help keep them warm.

Marsupials are a group of mammals that live mostly in Australia. Kangaroos, koalas, and wallabies are marsupials. They have a special pouch on their belly. When their babies are about the size of a caterpillar, they crawl into the pouch and attach to a mammary gland inside. They grow inside the pouch for several months. Even after leaving the pouch, the young mammals will return when they are hungry or scared.

This red-necked wallaby has a baby in its pouch. The baby has not grown fur yet.

Break the Rules

The platypus is a mammal that lives along the shores of streams in Australia. It has webbed feet with claws, a beaverlike tail, and a large, flat snout for scooping up worms and other small water creatures. A platypus is unusual because it lays eggs. Spiny anteaters and long-nosed echidnas lay eggs too.

This platypus is about to take a swim.

We Are Mammals

We are mammals, so we can often relate to other members of our group. Who can resist laughing at a monkey's antics? We all like to hold and pet puppies and kittens.

Other mammals are important sources of food and clothing. We raise cows for

Can you name the two mammals shown in this photograph?

Shearing

These people are cutting the
woolly coats off of two sheep.

milk and beef. Pigs provide pork chops and bacon. We make sweaters and mittens from the wool of sheep. The leather of our shoes and belts comes from animal hides.

Mammals are an important part of every ecosystem on Earth. Small mammals, such as mice and rabbits, are a source of food for hawks, eagles, snakes, and alligators. Lions, coyotes, and other

This red-tailed hawk has killed a squirrel and is about to eat it.

large mammals are hunters. By eating other creatures, these predators help keep animal populations from getting too big.

Because humans have very large brains, they have developed machines that help them do jobs faster and easier. A beaver using its teeth can only chop down a few trees a day.

Beavers use their large, sharp front teeth to cut down trees.

People can use
bulldozers to
knock down trees.

A person using a bulldozer can clear an entire forest in a few hours.

A cheetah kills one animal every few days. A person with a machine gun can kill an entire herd of animals in a few seconds.

As we clear land to build houses, roads, malls, and parking lots, we destroy the homes of hundreds of mammals. When a hunter kills an

How many animals do you think were killed to get this pile of tusks and horns?

elephant just for its tusks or a deer just for its antlers, he or she is wasting a life.

Mammals are the most intelligent group of animals, and humans are the most intelligent mammals. We know when we are hurting other animals, and we know that it is wrong.

Many animals already have disappeared from Earth forever and many more are in

Giant pandas are in danger because some people hunt and kill them.

danger. If we do not use our intelligence to work together to save other creatures, we will only be hurting ourselves. We cannot live without all of the other animals that share our planet.

To Find Out More

Here are some additional resources to help you learn more about mammals:

 **Books**

Brimner, Larry Dane. **Polar Mammals**. Children's Press, 1997.

Jansen, John and Susan Burke Slattery. **Playing Possum: Riddles About Kangaroos, Koalas, and Other Marsupials**. Lerner, 1995.

Landau, Elaine. **Desert Mammals.** Children's Press, 1997.

_____. **Grassland Mammals.** Children's Press, 1997.

Miller, Sara Swan. **Land Predators of North America.** Franklin Watts, 1999.

Patent, Dorothy Hinshaw. **Why Mammals Have Fur.** Cobble Hill Books, 1995.

Robinson, W. Wright. **Animal Architects: How Mammals Build Their Amazing Homes.** Blackbirch, 1999.

Stotsky, Sandra. **Amazing Mammals.** Chelsea House, 1999.

Sway, Marlene. **Bats: Mammals that Fly.** Franklin Watts, 1999.

Organizations and Online Sites

Hall of Mammals
*http://www.ucmp.berke-
ley.edu/mammal/mammal.
html*

Take a guided tour that will teach you many interesting facts about a variety of mammals.

The Marsupial Museum
*http://www.worldkids.net/
critters/marsupials/*

Learn all about cuscuses, kangaroos, quokkas, wombats, and other marsupials.

National Wildlife Federation
8925 Leesburg Pike
Vienna, VA 22184
http://www.nwf.org/

This group works to promote environmental education and to inspire and assist people to conserve our natural resources.

The Platypus
*http://www.schools.ash.org.
au/andcreek/platypus.htm*

Curious about platypuses? This entry is part of a larger site developed and maintained by students and teachers at the Anderson's Creek Primary School in Warrandyte, Australia.

Whale Songs
http://whales.ot.com/

Follow the experiences of an American science teacher who spends a week onboard *Song of the Whale*, a research vessel used to study whales and other ocean animals.

Important Words

canine tooth a pointed tooth used to rip or tear food

litter several animals born at one time to one mother

mammal a warm-blooded animal that feeds its young with mother's milk and usually has some hair covering its skin

mammary gland an organ on a female mammal's body that produces milk

marsupial a mammal that is born in an early stage of development and grows in its mother's pouch

molar a broad tooth with three points that is used to crush and grind food

predator an animal that kills and eats other animals for food

warm blooded having a body temperature that stays the same no matter how cold or warm it is outside

Index

Meet the Author

Melissa Stewart earned a Bachelor's Degree in biology from Union College and a Master's Degree in Science and Environmental Journalism from New York University. She has been writing about science and nature for almost a decade. Ms. Stewart lives in Danbury, Connecticut.